United States
Department of
Agriculture

Forest Service

Forest
Products
Laboratory

State and
Private Forestry

Technology
Marketing Unit

General
Technical
Report
FPL–GTR–168

Small-Diameter
Success Stories II

Jean Livingston

Abstract

Many of our national forests are in critical need of restoration. These forests are dense, with an abundance of small-diameter, tightly spaced trees and underbrush that can contribute to the rapid growth of fire. If economic and value-added uses for this small-diameter and unmerchantable material can be found, forest restoration costs could be offset and catastrophic wildfires would be reduced. This document tells the story of several U.S. wood product businesses that are successfully making use of this small-diameter and unmerchantable material. Some stories describe how the USDA Forest Service National Woody Biomass Grant Program is improving forest restoration by creating markets for this thinned material. One USDA Forest Service project in particular, the White Mountain Stewardship Contract, involves several wood product businesses that are receiving small-diameter and unmerchantable material and successfully producing value-added products.

Keywords: small-diameter timber, forest restoration, roundwood, small business, unmerchantable timber

April 2006

Livingston, Jean. 2006. Small-diameter success stories II. Gen. Tech. Rep. FPL-GTR-168. Madison, WI: U.S. Department of Agriculture, Forest Service, Forest Products Laboratory. 31 p.

A limited number of free copies of this publication are available to the public from the Forest Products Laboratory, One Gifford Pinchot Drive, Madison, WI 53726–2398. This publication is also available online at www.fpl.fs.fed.us. Laboratory publications are sent to hundreds of libraries in the United States and elsewhere.

The Forest Products Laboratory is maintained in cooperation with the University of Wisconsin.

Acknowledgment

I sincerely thank everyone who provided me with a personal interview and tour of their organization. The best part of my job is meeting all of you and possibly helping in some small way. Know that by sharing your story, you will help others.

Contents

Small-Diameter Success Stories II

Jean Livingston
USDA Forest Service
State & Private Forestry
Technology Marketing Unit
Forest Products Laboratory
One Gifford Pinchot Drive
Madison, WI 53726-2398

Foreword

In President Bush's 2006 State of the Union address he acknowledged that "… America is addicted to oil …" and set out a goal of replacing "… more than 75% of our oil imports from the Middle East by 2025." Wood chips are a part of this goal.

As a person who has spent more than 15 years on the issue of using small-diameter and low-valued trees that must be removed from our Federal lands to reduce the risk from catastrophic fire and insect and disease attacks, this endorsement is music to my ears. It took 15 years, a multitude of voices, and numerous catastrophic fires, but the issue has been raised.

However, with the President mentioning wood chips for biomass energy, we do not want to give the impression that the nation must start from ground zero. A considerable amount of progress has been made in those 15 years. But progress can be slow.

First, people had to recognize that we were talking about the "junk wood" in our forests. We were not talking about old growth or clear cuts but about removing the understory and opening up the canopy. Second, people had to discover that these treatments were very expensive; therefore, costs needed to be reduced. Third, people came to the realization that utilization might be a way to help reduce these costs. So people started discovering ways to use this "junk wood" to make products with economic value. Fourth, people had to understand that not all of this material was "junk." It may be small, but some of this material could be turned into flooring, paneling, and art work. If only 20% of the "junk wood" could be turned into higher valued products, it could help defray some of the forest treatment costs. We still need to find outlets such as biomass energy for the other 80%. Fifth, policies that emphasize these treatments on Federal lands needed to be established.

The Healthy Forest Restoration Act of 2003 and the Energy Policy Act of 2005 were passed, helping to focus the goals and roles of the Federal agencies. In addition, new authorities for stewardship contracts, which facilitated the exchange of goods for services, provided new ways of doing business for both the Bureau of Land Management and the USDA Forest Service. Sixth, we needed to implement some economic opportunities that help defray economic risk to small forest product businesses. The USDA Forest Service initiated the National Woody Biomass Utilization Grant Program. Thus, the stage was set.

This publication highlights some examples of the businesses and entrepreneurs that are making the program happen. These businesses are taking "junk" or low-value wood and helping to make a product—studs, pulp, poles, posts, flooring, molding, millwork, wood pellets, or biomass energy. They are creating and expanding businesses that are helping to restore our Federal forestlands. Whether the material comes from overstocked stands of small-diameter ponderosa pine or hurricane blow down from Katrina, these people are creating successes in using small-diameter and low-valued trees. This publication contains their stories.

As with the first publication of *Small-Diameter Success Stories*, by Jean Livingston, this document continues the stories of the energetic and indomitable spirit of the entrepreneurs who are committed to healthy forests and healthy rural communities. They have determination. They have passion. But most of all, they have commitment and do not give up, even when the barriers seem insurmountable. To these people, and to all others who are engaged in using small-diameter and underutilized wood, this publication is dedicated.

Susan LeVan-Green
Program Manager
State & Private Forestry
Technology Marketing Unit
USDA Forest Service
Forest Products Laboratory

Introduction

Many of our national forests have an abundance of small, tightly spaced trees and underbrush. This small-diameter and unmerchantable material has been left in the forest because either it is not economical to remove or local capacity to process such material does not exist. The dense material creates a ladder-type fuel that can lead to high-intensity fires that spread quickly. These types of fires can destroy entire stands of trees and cause major alterations to forested landscapes and watersheds.

Restoration of these overstocked stands, through mechanical thinning or prescribed burning, will remove most of the small-diameter material, thus helping the forest to recover its natural structure and ecological functions. Some of these forests are in a fire regime condition class 3, indicating that mechanical thinning is necessary prior to prescribed burning. However, mechanical forest thinning is extremely expensive. If new, economical, and value-added uses for thinned material can be found, forest restoration costs could be offset as the threat of catastrophic wildfires is reduced.

Wildland–urban interface project: White Mountain Stewardship contract before restoration.

Wildland–urban interface project: White Mountain Stewardship contract after restoration.

National Woody Biomass Utilization Grant Program

The National Woody Biomass Utilization Grant Program (administered by the USDA Forest Service State & Private Forestry Technology Marketing Unit, located at the Forest Products Laboratory, Madison, Wisconsin) is intended to help improve forest restoration activities on national forestlands by using and creating markets for small-diameter material and low-valued trees removed in hazardous fuel reduction activities. These funds are targeted to help communities, entrepreneurs, and others turn residues from hazardous fuel reduction projects into marketable forest products or biomass energy products.

The following are the goals of this grant program:

- Help reduce Forest Service management costs by increasing value of biomass and other forest products generated by hazardous fuel treatments.
- Create incentives or reduce business risk for increased use of biomass on national forestlands.
- Institute projects that target and help remove economic and market barriers to using small-diameter trees and woody biomass.

To help accomplish forest restoration, various approaches are being taken to complete the necessary work and simultaneously contribute to the economic growth of communities. Forestry agencies and many local forestry-dependent communities are partnering—working side by side—to find new ways of collaborative forest management, adapting to the opportunities and constraints offered by the ecosystem, and implementing new forest product technologies.

Restoration of our forests will persist as long as we continue working together for the ecological health of our forests and the economic health of forestry-based rural communities. This document tells the story of several wood product businesses and communities that are successfully making use of this small-diameter and unmerchantable material. Some stories describe how the USDA Forest Service's National Woody Biomass Utilization Grant Program (see sidebar) is working to improve forest restoration activities by helping to create markets from this thinned material. One USDA Forest Service project in particular, the White Mountain Stewardship Contract (see p. 21), involves several wood product businesses that are receiving small-diameter and unmerchantable material from a 10-year contract.

Dodge Logging, Inc.

Headquartered on the family ranch, Dodge Logging, Inc., is located outside of Maupin, Oregon, and it is truly a family affair with Dad, Mom, and their two sons and daughters-in-law all actively involved in the business. Richard Dodge, the Dad, has been active in the forest products industry for more than 30 years, and his wife, Janie, has been by his side all the way.

Starting in 1970 with just a chain saw and skidder, the Dodge family now owns and operates three mechanized logging operations; a stationary whole-log-ship and barge reload facility in Boardman, Oregon (Boardman Chip Company, Inc.); and a small-random-length dimension sawmill in Pendleton, Oregon (Blue Mountain Lumber Products, LLC).

The Dodge family is respected in the community and receives high praise from its project partners, in particular Morrow County. Richard prides himself in being a good steward of the land and has a long-time reputation for operating equipment that is "light on the land."

Maupin, in North Central Oregon, boasts that it is on the sunny side of Mt. Hood and one of Oregon's best kept secrets. This area is known for its white water rapids and wild trout and steelhead fishing on the Deschutes River.

Although home-based outside of Maupin, other Dodge family-owned companies are located in the Northeastern area of Oregon, where forest-thinning projects are challenged by rugged mountains, deep canyons, plateaus, and rolling hills. National Forests in this area include the Umatilla, Wallowa-Whitman, Mt. Hood, Ochoco, and Deschutes.

"Our company structure is lean," says Richard. Each company has an average of two people involved in day-to-day management, and most of these folks are working supervisors." All key personnel report to Richard, and final decisions are made through a committee consisting of the entire Dodge family in consultation with others if needed.

In 2005, Dodge Logging was awarded a grant for $250,000 from the USDA Forest Service National Woody Biomass Utilization Grant Program (see p. v) to upgrade and expand the small-diameter log processing capacity at their Boardman Chip Company.

The Boardman Chip Company is located near the Blue Mountains of northeast and central Oregon, where catastrophic wildfires are a common occurrence. The Dodge family understands the unhealthy forest situation in these regions and because of their unique enterprise—from logging to processing to marketing—are in an ideal position to contribute significantly to improving the health of several public and private forests in Oregon.

Richard notes that "Although we have already made substantial upgrades and equipment purchases to

Owners Richard and Janie Dodge.

improve forest thinning operations and processing facilities to increase the value of the material removed from the forest, we still did not have the ability to economically process logs that were less than 7-1/2 in. in diameter and to recover every log segment that might produce studs or lumber."

Improving recovery is important to the operating margin of a business. It also decreases the time and money spent by the USDA Forest Service for additional thinning treatments such as piling and burning.

Richard says they are expanding the small-diameter log processing capacity at the Boardman chip plant using funds from the 2005 National Woody Biomass Utilization Grant Program (see p. v). They hope to accomplish this within a year's time. As an end result, they will have increased the speed and automation to sort, merchandize, and process logs through a single-pass saw; improved the capacity of the twin-band at the Blue Mountain plant to handle oversized logs from the Boardman plant; upgraded material handling capacity at the Blue Mountain mill; and converted their outdated inventory and accounting system to a software package that will track and schedule their material from the log through lumber, chips, and residuals.

"This upgrade will result in what could be the first facility in the Intermountain West specially designed to accept and process mixed loads, meaning pulp logs but with a few small sawlog segments," noted Richard. "We also hope to eventually add a roundwood operation, a pellet manufacturing facility, and possibly a baled wood-shavings operation to supplement current residual markets."

Richard and Janie said that their business vision is "to grow and maintain a healthy, diversified family of forest products businesses for the long term." They intend to retain the 100 current jobs in the Dodge

Dodge Logging, Inc.
78888 Walters Road
Maupin, OR 97037

Dodge Logging, Inc., headquarters outside Maupin, Oregon.

companies and hope to add at least 10 more jobs as a result of their latest expansion.

There is no doubt that the Dodge Logging, Inc., will continue to build on their past successes, and one day the Dodge family will pass on to their children not only the Dodge family of companies, but their land stewardship ethics and sustainable forestry values as well.

Central Oregon Intergovernmental Council

The Central Oregon Intergovernmental Council (COIC) is an organization that helps businesses, residents, and communities in the central Oregon area. Since 1972, COIC has provided programs and services to the community such as employment and training, youth and adult education, business loans, and community and economic development.

One of COIC's projects, which was initially funded by the USDA Forest Service Economic Action Program in support of the National Fire Plan, is Central Oregon Partnerships for Wildfire Risk Reduction (COPWRR). This is a multi-stakeholder partnership with the ultimate goals of reducing forest wildfire risk, enhancing forest health, and providing community jobs in Central Oregon.

Scott Aycock, coordinator of the COPWRR project, explains the program:

"COPWRR was initiated to address the removal of dangerous build-up of woody biomass material in Central Oregon forests. Specific goals of COPWRR are to

• determine the long-term feasibility of using small-diameter logs and woody material to create wood products and produce energy,

• determine the best way to mechanically remove woody biomass from targeted forests, and

• develop a market-driven approach to hazardous fuel reduction that could maintain and create local jobs and bring differing stakeholders together in a common, sustainable resource direction."

In pursuing these goals, the COPWRR team learned through research that it is was critical to stabilize or "levelize" the supply of small-diameter material. They found that the wood supply on private and public forest lands has dramatically fluctuated for the past few years and that these fluctuations have contributed to a stall in technology investment and employment in the region.

Scott said that for planning purposes, forest products businesses need to be able to forecast a sufficient wood supply at least 5 to 10 years out. Small-diameter material is usually not managed as a resource, and it is very difficult to gather accurate data on its future supply.

These results lead the COPWRR team to work with numerous partners to implement a Coordinated Resource Offering Protocol (CROP) initiative. Developed by Catherine Mater of Mater Engineering, the CROP model coordinates small-diameter timber sales from multiple forests across large areas for 5, 10, and 15 years.

Catherine says this will "create a levelized supply of small trees, making logging them a more economically attractive proposition, especially for small companies that must rely on bank loans to finance their operations."

Central Oregon Intergovernmental Council headquarters, Redmond, Oregon.

In 2005, COIC was awarded a grant for $220,000 from the USDA Forest Service National Woody Biomass Utilization Grant Program (see p. *v*) to expand the CROP initiative.

By using CROP, these businesses are able to more accurately predict, achieve, and stabilize the wood supply, thus enabling them to invest in new technology and product development.

The CROP initiative is currently being applied across these public land agencies of Central Oregon: the Deschutes, Ochoco, and Mount Hood National Forests, the Prineville Bureau of Land Management, and the Confederated Tribes of Warm Springs.

Warm Springs Forest Products Industries, an enterprise on the reservation, is using CROP to help establish a 15-MW biomass power facility and a small-diameter timber processing line. Long-term supply is critical to the success of these biomass and processing facilities. Warm Springs can only supply 40,000 bone dry tons (bdt) from their mill waste. However, another 40,000 bdt has to come from off-reservation hazardous forest fuel reduction treatments, primarily from the Deschutes and Ochoco National Forests. Material used in the Warm Springs operations has to be sourced from 8,000 acres per year of forest fuel treatments. Currently, Warm Springs is able to pay only $10/bdt for very small-diameter biomass material. After installing their new facilities, estimates show that they can pay at least $20/bdt for the same material, equivalent to $100 to $200 per acre in reduced fuel treatment costs (assuming 10 to 20 bdt/acre). For 8,000 acres, this would result in a total treatment

Central Oregon
Intergovernmental Council
2363 SW Glacier Place
Redmond, OR 97756

Scott Aycock, Program Administrator.

savings of $800,000 to $1.6 million (source: Calvin Mukumoto, Warm Springs Consulting Forester).

Scott explains that each year CROP partners are creating detailed small-diameter supply projections from public and private lands within community supply landscapes, tailoring projections to the needs of individual users. Using Geographic Information System (GIS) analysis and other tools, conservative estimates of supply are created based on harvest costs, proximity to communities, and environmental and social factors. Partners also develop new data on harvesting and transportation costs and other local economic factors crucial to business investment decisions.

This information is communicated to local businesses, community groups, entrepreneurs, and the general public through forums, one-on-one meetings, and the internet. CROP partners gather feedback and make ongoing improvements. At the same time, COIC will continue to expand small-diameter utilization in the region by researching and developing small-diameter market opportunities and providing technical assistance to new businesses.

According to Scott, "We anticipate that the levelization of small-diameter timber supply through the CROP project will have long-term (20+ years) positive impacts in terms of costs per acre, increases in acres treated, and community jobs. It is part of a long-term program to develop a new forest-based economy in rural Central Oregon, based in part on forest restoration activities, and is expected to hatch as a self-sustaining local initiative at the conclusion of the 2-year pilot project term."

The CROP initiative is now being looked at as a project that could be implemented nationally. COIC definitely has the technical expertise, skills, and history of working with Central Oregon forest management stakeholders to implement this project. We look forward to watching the successful progress of this program.

North Slope Sustainable Wood, LLC

In 2002, four unlikely partners came together to form North Slope Sustainable Wood, LLC, in Missoula, Montana. The company offers random-length tongue-and-groove flooring made from western larch logs harvested from forest restoration projects throughout the Northern Rocky Mountains.

Peter Stark, an outdoor and adventure writer, owned 80 forested acres of western larch and fir in Missoula's Rattlesnake Valley. Those 80 acres needed restoration. So when Peter's wife, Amy Ragsdale, also noted that she was in need of a professional dance floor to facilitate her dance instruction profession, Peter hired Matt Arno, a professional restoration forester, to thin their 80 heavily forested acres.

Maybe it was the cost of the professional dance floor that triggered Peter to wonder if there was a higher valued use for the small-diameter trees being removed than selling them for a very low cost to a local paper mill. We will never know for sure, but these questions lead Peter to research and subsequently discover that the harvested small-diameter larch could possibly be made into a high-valued wood flooring. Peter then hired a company to custom saw, dry, and mill the logs into high-valued flooring.

Next, Peter hired Shannon O'Keefe, a local professional flooring contractor, to install the beautiful, tight-grain larch floor in Amy's new dance studio. Stark, owner of the logs, Arno who actually thinned the forest, and Shannon, who laid the flooring, were extremely pleased with the quality of Amy's dance floor. In fact, they showcase Amy's dance floor in their business, highlighting the value and benefits of utilizing forest restoration material.

In their final move, these three men contacted Mike Wood, a forester and a lawyer with an extensive background in environmental issues and "green-certification" procedures. Mike saw the possibilities, joined the other three as the fourth partner, and North Slope Sustainable Wood, LLC, was born.

Mike notes, "Western larch, or tamarack, has a long tradition in Europe as a superior and beautiful flooring, with its dense, honey-colored grain and dark pinhole knots. Our western larch is unique to the Northern Rockies. In our region, it typically grows on mid-elevation north-facing slopes—sites with light to moderate annual precipitation."

Wood flooring has a prime market when cut from high-quality hardwood and softwood species. Although hardwood species are generally more popular as a flooring material, higher density softwood species are also used. Softwood species regularly manufactured into flooring include southern pine, Douglas-fir, western hemlock, and western larch.

Owners of North Slope Sustainable Wood, LLC.

Amy's dance floor.

Some literature erroneously suggests that wood cut from small-diameter trees is weaker than wood cut from large-diameter trees. USDA Forest Service research has established that the properties of wood from small-diameter trees may be just as good as those cut from large-diameter trees.

There is considerable interest in how the properties of such material compares with those traditionally assumed for western

North Slope Sustainable
    Wood, LLC
P.O. Box 8846
Missoula, MT 59807

Larch flooring installed in Forest Service employee Angela Farr's home, Missoula, Montana.

softwood species. The physical and mechanical properties of small-diameter trees thinned from overstocked stands are dependent upon species, the age of the tree, and the conditions under which the tree is growing.

As part of a USDA Forest Service evaluation of utilization options for wood harvested from forest thinning projects, the Forest Products Laboratory evaluated the hardness of two species currently being used in the West for finished flooring—Douglas-fir and western larch. Several Douglas-fir 2 by 4s were obtained from suppressed growth trees in northern California, and western larch flooring was provided by North Slope Sustainable Wood, LLC. The larch flooring was cut from suppressed, small-diameter trees growing in Montana.

Results indicate that the suppressed Douglas-fir had 22% to 44% greater-than-species-average hardness values commonly assumed for Douglas-fir. The western larch results were about 6% greater than values commonly assumed for larch.

"As word has spread about our company, sales have steadily increased over the past year. We're still operating on a fairly small scale, but it has actually been good for us and is allowing us to work out the small glitches in our processing and delivery," Mike says.

Sometimes when the most unlikely group of people come together, the best is accomplished. In the case of North Slope Sustainable Wood, this is definitely true.

Mount Wachusett Community College

Mount Wachusett Community College has become a leader in promoting and demonstrating woody biomass as a sustainable and renewable energy source. Built in 1974, the college's main campus is located on 280 acres in Gardner, Massachusetts, and has about 450,000 square feet of buildings that need to be lighted, heated, and cooled.

The college campus was initially an all-electric system, and their utility bills over the years have skyrocketed, exceeding $750,000 per year. In 1996, a study was funded to find possible solutions to reduce their high energy costs.

Results of the college's study indicated a possible conversion to a biomass-fired hydronic system, utilizing woody biomass fuel. The plan indicated a possible annual savings of $276,000, with a simple payback on investment (excluding financing) in about 9 years. Wood residue material from local sawmills could meet the college's long-term supply needs.

The plan was adopted, and in April 2002 Mount Wachusett Community College began constructing a new wood biomass heating system that came on line for the 2002–2003 heating season, replacing the existing all-electric system. This new system is saving the college an estimated $300,000 per year.

Rob Rizzo, Director of Facilities Administration at the college, said, "Over the past several years, we have implemented a variety of energy conservation measures including variable air volume conversion, installation of variable frequency drives on air-handling units, chiller replacements, new energy-efficient lighting, heat pumps, cooling tower replacement, domestic hot water conversion, replacement of unit ventilators, and the installation of a new domestic hot water heat exchanger. These additional energy conservation measures have reduced our total electrical consumption to approximately 8 million kWH at a cost of approximately $670,000."

Building on its commitment to use woody biomass as a sustainable and renewable energy source, the college recently partnered with Community Power Corporation (CPC) to build and install a 50 kW downdraft gasifier (BioMax™), using wood chips as the feedstock. Located in Littleton, Colorado, CPC develops, commercializes, and markets modular biopower systems to meet the needs of distributed energy consumers in both nondeveloped and developed countries. The BioMax™ 50 will provide heat, air conditioning, and electricity for the college's newly constructed daycare center. This will be CPC's first installation of a BioMax™ 50.

The college hopes to have the BioMax™ 50 in operation at their daycare center by April 2006. Plans are to have Rob Rizzo oversee this project and provide the technology transfer to help bring it from the demonstration stage to commercialization.

Mount Wachusett Community College's biomass power plant.

"So far, Mount Wachusett Community College is the only state agency to switch to a biomass heating plant, a technology that's been in use in other states for about three decades," said Rob.

Rob also noted that the biomass plant has not only saved the college money. By cutting utility bills, the college has been able to keep student fees steady for the past 3 years. College President Daniel Asquino estimates that the decreased costs of operating a biomass heating plant has saved the average student about $400 a year in fees.

The college has indeed reversed the old proverb "practice what you preach" and turned it into "preach what you practice." The college is in the process of developing an associate degree program in renewable energy and technology. Right now Rob has developed three courses on renewable technologies, and these classes were offered for the first time in the Spring 2006 semester.

Rob acknowledges that "Support from many sources has made all this possible. One of the strongest supporters has been Massachusetts Congressman John Olver, who was able to secure funding to help complete the energy conservation measures at the college. Executive Vice-President Ed Terceiro coordinated and implemented the entire program, and College President Dan Asquino had the vision and supplied the guidance and leeway to move forward with these projects."

In 2005, the college received the "Excellence in Energy Efficiency" award from the Commonwealth of Massachusetts. In the past 3 years, the college has reduced their greenhouse gas emissions by 18½%, which is a phenomenal number. Rob remarks, "Our President has gone on record to say that the college will have a minimum of a 25% reduction of greenhouse gas emissions by 2012."

Mount Wachusett
Community College
444 Green Street
Gardner, MA 01440-1000

Woodchip boiler inside the biomass power plant.

The college began by wanting to cut its energy costs and now has progressed to becoming an authority on sustainable and renewable energy. Their goals have evolved into reducing greenhouse gas emission levels, teaching students about renewable energy sources, and helping to advance woody biomass as a viable energy option. Mount Wachusett Community College is definitely living up to its motto, "Education for a Changing World."

Northwest Wood Products Association

Located in Bend, Oregon, Northwest Wood Products Association (NWPA) is a private, non-profit trade association for secondary wood products manufacturers. The association provides assistance to their members in market development, capital access, technology and training, and supply development. Their 80 members are primarily from the Pacific Northwest.

Dennis Brock, Executive Director for NWPA, provides some statistics on the secondary wood products industry. "In 1990, it maintained about 19% of the employment in the wood products industry. In 2003, the secondary wood products industry retained 37% to 46% of Oregon's overall employment in the wood products industry and sometimes as much as 63% in the rural communities." Dennis strongly believes, "The wood products industry is not dying—it's just changing."

According to Dennis, "In 1990, 1 million board feet of raw exported log timber created one job. Today, in the secondary wood products industry, that same million board feet can create as many as 24 jobs." Dennis believes there are unlimited opportunities for the secondary wood products industry in Oregon.

As mentioned, supply development is a major function of NWPA. One recent project of NWPA's involved partners that included the USDA Forest Service, the Oregon Economic and Community Development Department, and the city of Fossil, Oregon. This project was designed to establish part of the new infrastructure needed to process small-diameter and underutilized species in Central Oregon. Installing a small-capacity dry kiln center became an integral part of this new infrastructure.

Data from this small-capacity drying system are helping establish proper drying schedules, cycle times, and other technical information needed to continue developing this new infrastructure. With this knowledge, the wood products industry is able to maximize nontraditional (e.g., juniper) and small-diameter species such as lodgepole pine, white fir, Douglas-fir, and ponderosa pine.

Large capacity kiln dryers are not suited for drying small-diameter timber, and most mills in Oregon that have large dryers have closed their doors. However, a large quantity of wood fiber is available from national forests and state and private forests. Estimates claim that over the next 20 years, about 880,000 acres of our national forests are scheduled to be thinned. The placement of a small-capacity dryer close to the timber resource reduces added transportation, processing, and drying costs for wood products manufacturers.

For example, wood harvested in a central Oregon community would have to be transported to another town to have it kiln-dried, the dried wood would then have to be

Dennis Brock, Executive Director, Northwest Wood Products Association.

transported back to central Oregon for manufacturing. This process alone could add $300 to $350 per thousand board feet to a company's processing costs.

In June 1993, NWPA applied for and received a USDA Forest Service grant to install a small-capacity dryer in Fossil's new industrial park. In January 2004, the Oregon Economic and Community Development provided additional funding. The dry kiln is accessible to local manufacturers and individuals producing wood products. Several potential users signed up early for the service so that this drying facility could process trees removed from eight of Oregon's eastern counties.

The city of Fossil agreed to provide space in their newly developed industrial park. The city was also instrumental in securing grant funding to erect a new building to house the dry kiln. Local business owner Tim Coe and Brunt Ranch Juniper, located in Fossil, agreed to provide day-to-day management of the operation in return for reduced kiln drying charges. Although this project encountered numerous delays and challenges along the way, an open house for the dryer was held in July 2005.

The NWPA posts on their website all current information pertaining to the small-capacity dryer. Appropriate drying schedules for the dry kiln were determined with the support of Scott Leavengood, Oregon State University, and Paul Dailey, Dailey Wood Products in Reedsport, Oregon. Refinement of the process and modified drying schedules is continuing to be updated and shared on NWPA's website.

This small-capacity dryer project is just one of NWPA's many projects. Dennis notes, "NWPA is continuing to fulfill its original purpose of

Northwest Wood Products Association
18900 Riverwoods Drive
Bend, OR 97701

Small-capacity wood dryer in Fossil, Oregon.

helping wood products manufacturers grow and become more profitable by helping them make connections to new markets, locate financing opportunities, take advantage of employee training programs, and find alternate sources of supply."

The NWPA is a true believer in partnerships between private and public sectors and understands that this is a key element to successful job creation and community sustainability and profitability. Their mantra is, "Private industry can't do it alone. Education can't do it alone. Government can't do it alone. Together we are stronger."

P&M Signs, Inc.

Phil Archuletta is an entrepreneur "extraordinaire." In addition to being an author, inventor, and community activist, he is the successful CEO of P&M Signs, Inc., and its sister companies P&M Plastics and P&M Small Timber Processing—all located in Mountainair, New Mexico. These for-profit companies are dedicated to "the recycling of forest residues in exchange for the creation of jobs in economically deprived communities."

Combined, the P&M companies employ 17 full-time employees, with a total experience of more than 75 years of creating high-quality signs. In 2004, P&M sales were about $1.8 million with a payroll of about $30,000 per month. Phil calculates that the family of P&M companies has a $3.6 million annual economic impact on the community.

Located adjacent to the Cibola National Forest, Mountainair is a rural community of about 1,300. Average household income is $25,651 per year, and the community has a 9.6% unemployment rate. The spread of western juniper and pinyon pine in this area has created millions of acres of small-diameter woodlands, resulting in problems such as lowering the water table, reducing rangeland, and creating severe erosion, which pollutes streams and lakes.

When Phil arrived in Mountainair in 1991, he had only $300 in his pocket, but he had a "can do" attitude and more than 30 years of experience in sign manufacturing. He had also spent 15 years working with the Missoula Technology Development Center on a durability study for signs while serving as Secretary-Treasurer for Ojo Caliente Craftsmen in northern New Mexico. As a result of his work experience, perseverance, and a little bit of luck, he opened P&M Signs, Inc., in 1991, and his business is now the largest employer in the area.

Phil knew that finding an economic use for western juniper and pinyon pine from these woodlands would alleviate some of the environmental problems associated with them. This area is also extremely vulnerable to forest wildfire as a result of the dense juniper and pine and a very dry climate. Reducing hazardous forest fuels is a priority in this area; however, the lack of local markets for small-diameter material is a limitation.

Historically, western juniper has been used for firewood and fence posts, but the high costs of harvesting and processing have limited attempts to develop and utilize it further. Even commercial firewood operations are only marginally successful because of the labor-intensive nature of harvesting, and the relative availability and low cost of steel posts and treated timber have diminished the practicality of using juniper for posts.

To reverse these trends, Phil developed a strategy to increase the value of the resource, primarily by

Phil T. Archuletta, CEO, P&M Signs, Inc.

Dense juniper and pine in a very dry climate.

developing products of higher value. One of those products is Altree™—a wood–plastic composite that has high value and has been a success for this company and the community.

Phil led the effort to develop Altree™ in collaboration with the USDA Forest Service Forest Products Laboratory and other agencies and groups. Now listed on government contract, Altree™ is so named because all parts of the tree are utilized—the bark, branches, needles, and berries. Made from small-diameter western juniper and pinyon pine trees and recycled plastic containers, Altree™ is non-corrosive, insect and mold resistant, nontoxic, and stable in all weather conditions.

To increase the product's success, Altree™ has been designated as a USDA "biobased" product. Biobased products are those commercial and industrial non-food products that are made, in whole or a significant part, of biological or renewable domestic agricultural or forestry materials. The Federal Biobased Products Preferred Procurement

P&M Signs, Inc.
202 E. Broadway
P.O. Box 567
Mountainair, NM 87036-0567

First Lady Laura Bush's Preserve America sign.

Program (http://www.biobased.oce.usda.gov/public/index.cfm) requires all Federal agencies to develop an affirmative procurement program for purchasing USDA-designated biobased products. Analysts expect that the future biobased market could be worth several billions of dollars.

Altree™ can be used for signage, plaques, decking, fencing and railing, spindles and posts, picnic tables, sandboxes, trash can holders, park benches, window boxes, tool handles, shims, window boxes, landscape timbers, and grading stakes and in marine and waterproofing situations in place of treated plywood and pressboard.

Major customers of Altree™ include the USDA Forest Service, New Mexico Highway Department, New Mexico State Parks, New Mexico Game and Fish, and National Parks.

Two Altree™ customers from the USDA Forest Service are Phil Bono, Six Rivers National Forest in California, and Vicky Estrada, Mountainair Ranger District. Estrada says that "We have used the Altree™ signs for the past 4 years. P&M Signs has always been very responsive to our requests, completing and delivering on time, and has been an extraordinary positive partner in developing uses for our small-diameter western juniper and pine trees. Altree™ has proven to be resistant to weather, gun shots, and porcupines."

So next time you drive through a national forest, pay particular attention to the signs on the roads and trails. You may see the attractive and durable Altree™ signs produced by P&M Signs, Inc., made from recycled plastic and the invasive western juniper and pine.

Altree™ is not P&M Signs' only product. They can produce signage to any requested specifications. Phil said, "We even have a crew that will hang the outdoor signs, if asked." Right now, building a large-scale Altree™ processing plant (100 by 200 feet) is one of the company's goals, which they hope to achieve by summer 2006. Most of the equipment has been purchased; they just need to construct the building.

Another P&M goal is to open a sawmill operation, using an existing building to produce vigas, latillas, and other pole products in addition to sawn lumber. Between the new Altree™ processing plant and the sawmill, 65 more jobs could be available in the community.

In November 2005, Phil was notified that P&M Signs was awarded a 5-year, exclusive Smokey Bear licensing agreement. Phil said "I've been trying for 35 years to get this license. Printing an icon like Smokey Bear is an incredible opportunity for us."

Smokey Bear signs will be printed in full color using a high-density reflective sheeting material developed by Phil. This material has proven to last for years and not lose its reflective capabilities. According to Phil, "We are bringing Smokey back to New Mexico, his first home. We plan to launch a huge Smokey Bear campaign all across the country." (The first Smokey Bear was rescued from a fire near Capitan, New Mexico, in 1950.)

Smokey Bear sign made using Altree™ and coated with high-density reflective sheeting.

Phil also competed and won the contract to print the signage for First Lady Laura Bush's Preserve America initiative. This initiative is an effort to encourage and help fund community efforts for the preservation and enjoyment of America's priceless cultural and natural heritage. To date, more than 220 communities in 37 states have received this designation. Each community is required to order the official Preserve America logo signs from P&M Signs.

Phil has a vast network of contacts—from local to national—and he is very active in his community. The following is only a short list of his awards and accomplishments.

- USDA National Most Successful Minority Owned Business
- SBA New Mexico Advisory Board Chairman
- Small Business Association Regional Award
- Mountainair City Council Member
- Mountainair Chamber of Commerce, President
- Green Zia Quality Award

Phil Archuletta cares deeply about people and especially his community. This entrepreneur "extraordinaire" continues to have a successful future in the wood products business. The only problem is keeping pace with his ingenious ideas, his energetic company goals, and his dynamic aspirations for the community.

Pomegranate Center

The Pomegranate Center is not a small-diameter wood business—it is a community-based nonprofit dedicated to social and environmental issues. The Center develops creative ways to achieve its goals; finds positive and sustainable solutions to problems; and works on projects in partnership with government and other public agencies. Located in Issaquah, Washington (near Seattle), the Pomegranate Center was incorporated in 1986 by Milenko Matanovic, Executive Director.

Milenko is a professional artist and community organizer. "I was concerned with the direction of modern communities, so I created the Pomegranate Center to explore how artists can have a role outside the narrow artistic world and be actively involved in building better communities."

The Pomegranate Center helps individuals use their talents to improve their communities. They do this by integrating social, artistic, and environmental viewpoints into "creating meaningful gathering spaces, initiating inclusive community-based planning, and providing educational outreach, research, and training."

Milenko explained further: "We plan and design gathering places, parks, neighborhood focal points, community trails, and public artworks that contribute to the community. Studies show that well-designed public spaces contribute to a stronger sense of community, good relations between neighbors, and feelings of safety and security. In our own experience, factors such as community distinction, cultural vitality, and social interaction are also greatly enhanced. These attributes are important not only to residents, but to policymakers, housing developers, lenders, and neighboring communities."

The Pomegranate Center facilitates public forums and town meetings, helping communities identify common concerns and objectives, discover creative methods of attaining goals, and find positive, sustainable solutions to problems. "Our programs reinforce civic connection and commitment, train local residents to solve problems, and create long-term leadership capacity within a community to meet future needs."

Their community-based planning projects are collaborative efforts between government agencies, non-profit organizations, architects, landscape architects, artists, developers, and community builders interested in public involvement processes. Their Gathering Places program focuses on affordable housing communities and neighborhoods in need of civic focal points. Affordable housing communities consisting of recent immigrants and refugees often provide the location for Pomegranate projects.

Milenko says their work proactively responds to the steady decline of community life. Rapid societal change and its byproducts (sprawl, traffic congestion, and environmental degradation) have lead to a loss of pride and sense of community and decreased participation in activities that support local vitality.

In 2000, the Pomegranate Center received a grant to study the social conditions of Springwood Apartments (Kent, Washington), one of the largest subsidized housing projects in the state of Washington. Based on their findings, the Center developed a plan to revitalize outdoor spaces that would provide a focal point for the entire community, where individuals from the community could provide hands-on construction and stimulate interaction among those living in the community.

Then in 2002, the USDA Forest Service awarded a grant to the Pomegranate Center to explore the use of small-diameter roundwood to revitalize Springwood's outdoor spaces. They constructed two mailbox shelters (10 by 36 feet and 10 by 24 feet) and a 10- by 8-feet kiosk where the Springwood community could post information and children could display their artwork. The suppressed-growth Douglas-fir 4- to 5-in.-diameter roundwood used had been harvested from a restoration project on a local smartwood tree farm in Shelton, Washington.

Since Springwood, the Pomegranate Center has also been exploring the use of roundwood as a viable construction material in creating outdoor facilities in two other low-income housing projects: Riverwalk Point in Spokane and Benson East in Kent. So far, they have renovated a playground and designed and built two mailbox shelters, kiosks, light posts, entry signs, a bus shelter, numerous tables and benches, a tea shelter, and fencing. Again, these projects were assisted through a grant from the USDA Forest Service, and the roundwood used in the projects was harvested from forest restoration projects.

Milenko commented, "We enjoy exploring the different uses for small-diameter roundwood because not only are we helping to add vibrancy to the outdoor spaces of numerous communities in need, we are contributing to the health of our forests."

The Pomegranate Center plans to continue playing a part in finding uses for small-diameter roundwood material harvested from forest restoration projects. Their goal is to partner with someone who will mass-produce the roundwood products Pomegranate has designed and used in their projects.

Pomegranate Center
P.O. Box 486
1400 NW Maple Street
Issaquah, WA 98027

Pomegranate projects: entry signs, mailbox shelters, light posts, tables and benches, tea shelter, and a bus shelter.

Santa Clara Woodworks

Santa Clara, New Mexico, is fortunate to have an involved and vital member of the community like Gordon West. Gordon owns Santa Clara Woodworks, a "woodworking and fabrication business dedicated to the production of quality products from locally obtained materials in a manner that promotes good stewardship of the land and support of the community."

Gordon started his first business, Gordon West Joinery, in 1977 in Missoula, Montana. In 1982, he moved his company to northern Idaho, then in 1997 to Santa Clara, New Mexico, and renamed it Santa Clara Woodworks. Gordon came to New Mexico with 20 years of experience in carpentry, sawmilling, and logging; his plan was to focus on building log cabins made from small-diameter logs.

Santa Clara, formerly called Central City, is located 6 miles east of Silver City on U.S. Highway 180. Santa Clara covers 1 square mile and has a population of about 2,000, primarily Hispanic. It is the oldest village in the district and its history is closely tied to nearby Fort Bayard. This buffalo-soldier fort sprung up in 1866 and played an integral role in protecting settlers and those in the nearby mining districts.

Situated in Grant County, Santa Clara is nestled in the foothills of the Pinos Altos Mountains. It borders the Continental Divide and is very close to the Gila National Forest. As a result of low copper prices and the forces of the international economy on the border industries, approximately 1,200 jobs have been lost in the local mining industry and supporting sectors. In addition, two local sawmills have closed in the past 10 years, because of a lack of a reliable supply of saw logs. Statistics show unemployment levels have exceeded 12%.

Santa Clara proved to be no different than any other place Gordon has lived. Shortly after arriving, he soon found out that the supply that he wanted was not available when he tried to obtain logs to continue his log home business. However, the nearby 3.3 million acres of Gila National Forest faced, and continues to pose, a high risk of catastrophic wildfire because of an overabundance of dense, overstocked forest stands. So, to obtain a small-diameter wood supply, Gordon partnered with two organizations and helped them complete a 16-acre restoration project on the Gila National Forest.

Wherever Gordon has lived, he has been involved with local businesses and environmental groups to promote appropriate public and private forestry and to use the wood from these efforts to create wood product businesses. Over the years, Gordon has become known for his forward thinking, successful collaboration efforts, and strong forestry stewardship principles.

In 1999, he and Todd Schulke from the Center for Biological Diversity founded Gila WoodNet. Gordon says, "Their

Gordon West, owner of Santa Clara Woodworks.

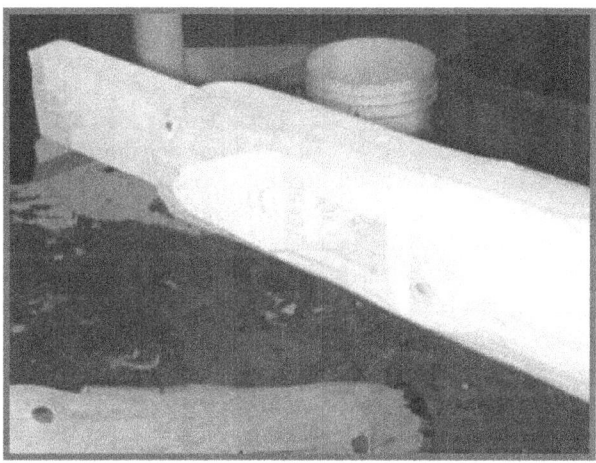

Hand-peeled and notched small-diameter poles are used in log cabins, allowing natural logs to be used in traditional timber frame construction.

vision of forest restoration meshed with my logging equipment and forestry techniques, but the scale of Santa Clara Woodworks operations was too small to achieve landscape-scale results in the forest."

Gila WoodNet, located in Santa Clara's Industrial Park, is a non-profit corporation associated with many wood businesses that perform forest restoration work. WoodNet operates a small log-sort yard and processing operation, which creates a biomass wood supply for small wood businesses and new jobs for the community. Gila Wood-Net directly employs 6 people. Most of the start-up costs for Gila WoodNet were obtained through grant funds from the Ford Foundation and USDA Forest Service programs.

Gordon noted, "Twenty percent of the woody biomass from forest restoration projects is useful for high-value

Santa Clara Woodworks
4100 N. Gold Street
Silver City, NM 88061

Chipcrete, a chip-based composite structural building block.

products and 80% is not. This 20% produces 80% of the business complex's revenue." All profits from Gila WoodNet are put back into forest restoration work and product development. Products from the company currently include vigas, poles, juniper posts, firewood, mulch, and chips.

Although it's a different way to look at it, Gordon figures that "Gila WoodNet creates one full-time job directly related to wood for every 10 restored forest acres. Gila WoodNet has a target of treating 300 acres per year in mechanical forest restoration. About 10,000 forest acres are qualified for mechanical thinning within 50 miles of Santa Clara. That would give Gila WoodNet a 30-year plan of restoring 300 acres per year."

Gordon said, "Now that GilaWoodNet is up and operating and has a supply of ethically sourced logs, I am resuming my efforts through Santa Clara Woodworks to develop buildings and products utilizing small-diameter trees. I want to focus on maximizing added value while minimizing product costs and to promote small-diameter roundwood as a standard building material."

Santa Clara Woodworks is a one-employee business. Rather than hiring employees, Gordon prefers to have what he labels "collaborators." He does not always have continual work for employees, so he works with a collaboration of partners to get the job done, and he actively seeks other woodworkers and craftspeople to share future projects.

Some of the small-diameter wood products that Gordon has adapted or developed over the years include log cabins, trusses, timber frames, furniture, structural composite blocks, and erosion-control material.

His log cabins are built using hand-peeled and notched small-diameter poles. The styles reflect early USDA Forest Service guard stations and National Park Service structures. For his trusses, he uses a unique Center Line System Log Joint-Making Tool that he invented and fabricated.

Because of this method, all parts are interchangeable between trusses, which makes it easier for later on-site log cabin assembly. In addition, the joint-making tool allows natural logs to be used in traditional timber frame construction.

One product still in development is Chipcrete, a chip-based composite structural building block, partially funded under a USDA grant. An erosion-control material called Zerosion is a spin-off of Chipcrete. Zerosion uses the lowest valued part of woody biomass and can be engineered for a wide variety of site-specific conditions.

To do small-diameter forest restoration projects, Gordon explains that you need multi-functional equipment. "For the scale that we and several other communities want to work at, there is no equipment or infrastructure appropriate to that scale. The equipment is either too small or too big, and we have to modify it to make it work." To fill in this equipment gap, Gordon built a light-on-the-land, 36-hp small-log forwarder that uses a small crane. He has subsequently attached a larger crane and is using the small crane as an attachment on the bobcat used in the yard.

Gordon also has developed a simple solar heat collector and has installed a solar dry kiln onsite. "Ponderosa pine is difficult to drawknife if it is wet, so we debark and sticker-stack our logs to air dry or use our solar-dry kiln if necessary."

Gordon has developed or modified other equipment, including bobcat log attachments, winch systems, and a Unilogger. Early on, his business was focused on construction so it was natural to modify equipment already in service to do the small-scale logging needed to get a supply of wood.

"Using a one-ton truck with log bunks, pulling a trailer with the Bobcat outfitted with a yarding winch attachment, two people can go to the forest in the morning and come home in the early afternoon with enough wood to keep busy for a week on a cabin or truss order," says West.

At the shop, a set of grapple forks for the Bobcat helps to move logs around efficiently. Recently, Gordon conducted a fabrication workshop with forest workers from northern New Mexico and Colorado, helping them to make their own winch attachments. The Unilogger is an improved version of the earlier small forwarder. It is a Mercedes-Benz Unilog truck heavily modified to be a cut-to-length feller, a three-winch mobile cable yarder, and a low-impact forwarder, all in one. It would also be possible to use the Unilogger to haul loads from the forest to the sortyard, although Gila WoodNet will use it as a dedicated forestry machine. West expects it to boost the pace of restoration

Unilogger, an improved version of the earlier small forwarder.

thinning; felling, limbing, bucking, and forwarding several hundred trees per day with a crew of two.

Gordon is involved with wood-related organizations and businesses throughout the region and feels that these contacts have great potential for developing new wood products and markets. In addition to Gila WoodNet, he works in collaboration with organizations that help with research and development of new wood products, innovative craft furniture makers, other decorative wood products, and a timber framer. He recently started a consulting business with several others in the region, Rural Business Implementation Group (RBIG), with a mission of actively assisting other communities to establish robust and diverse wood industries based on forest restoration.

Clearly this community has gained a valuable human resource by the name of Gordon West. He has a passionate land ethic and strong community-based values. Gordon has had a positive influence on the community, as seen by the increasing number of wood-based jobs and businesses created from forest-restoration thinning projects. We look forward to seeing more of Gordon's ideas on equipment development, his innovation in creating small-diameter wood products, and his forward thinking applied for the betterment of this community.

It's easy to find—Warm Springs Forest Products Industries (WSFPI) is just off to your right on Highway 26 as you pass north through the town of Warm Springs, which is in the north-central part of Oregon.

In 1967, the Confederated Tribes of the Warm Springs Reservation purchased Jefferson Plywood Corporation and established Warm Spring Forest Products Industries. With each having their distinctive heritage, the tribes of Warm Springs, Wasco, and Northern Paiute make up the Confederated Tribes of Warm Springs. The reservation consists of about 640,000 acres, half forested, between the Cascade Crest and the Deschutes River. The Deschutes, Mt. Hood, Ochoco, and Willamette National Forests either border or are adjacent to the reservation. There are more than 4,000 Tribal members and most live in or around the town of Warm Springs.

The Tribal economy here is based primarily on natural resources (hydropower, forest products, ranching), tourism, and recreation. With high unemployment rates (about 17% in summer and 35% in winter), the reservation struggles with economic development. The Tribes have always strived to develop sustainable businesses aligned with the environment and their culture.

Larry Potts, CEO of Warm Springs Forest Products Industries, said, "We harvest nearly 42 million board feet of timber per year. Species include incense cedar, ponderosa pine, white pine, lodgepole pine, Douglas-fir, western larch, noble fir, grand fir, and white fir." They maximize the return to the Tribe while using the raw material in an efficient and environmentally sound way. Most of their harvest is used in the manufacturing process; however, some logs are sold on the open market.

Warm Springs Forest Products Industries produces Douglas-fir, white fir, and ponderosa pine framing and industrial lumber and timbers, 4- by 4-in. through 12- by 12-in., in lengths of 8 and 20 feet. All framing and industrial lumber products are dried, planed, and graded under the industry standard rules and regulations of the Western Wood Products Association. WSFPI is also certified by Forest Stewardship Council (FSC), which is an international non-profit organization devoted to encouraging responsible management of the world's forests.

Larry explains that the Tribal Council feels that "a strategy to provide jobs and revenue while in concert with reducing fuels from the forest is possible by producing biomass energy."

Warm Springs Forest Products Industries P.O. Box 810 3270 Highway 26 Warm Springs, OR 97761

Warm Springs Forest Products Industries currently operates a biomass power plant. However, it is antiquated and inefficient.

Larry Potts, CEO, Warm Springs Forest Products Industries.

They have a three-phase plan to improve and enlarge their biomass energy plant and upgrade their capacity to process small-diameter logs.

Phase I, completed in September 2005, replaced the plant's 1927 boilers. Phase II replaces the current limited-use condensing turbine with an extraction turbine that is much more conducive to a sawmill operation. The WSFPI plans to use the steam produced to dry lumber and double their power production. The new boiler (Phase I) combined with the condensing turbine is capable of producing up to 3 MW of power. With the new larger extraction turbine, they could produce an additional 6 MW of power.

Phase III plans include installing a small-diameter (5- to 7-in. diameter) log processor and adding a second boiler and turbine. Their current mill can only efficiently process logs greater than 8-in. diameter. The new small-log facility could provide 20 new jobs. When the second boiler is added, WSFPI could potentially have 15 to 20 MW of power for sale or internal use.

Larry added, "The Tribe is actively reviewing a proposal to sell PacifiCorp, our utility provider, the renewable energy they produce. We want to be part of the solution of utilizing woody biomass material."

In 2005, a grant for $250,000 from the USDA Forest Service National Woody Biomass Utilization Grant Program (see p. v)
to help with Phase II of their project was "extremely appreciated and helpful toward completion of our three-phase biomass energy strategy," noted Larry.

As a result of completing Phase II using the National Woody Biomass Utilization Grant, WSFPI hopes to increase the current price it pays for delivered woody biomass from off-reservation sources, such as the national forests that surround their land. The increase in price paid would help offset the cost of harvesting these fuels.

Office of Warm Springs Forest Products Industries.

Right now, WSFPI can supply only 40,000 bone dry tons (bdt) of biomass from their mill waste. They plan to purchase the remaining 40,000 bdt needed from off-reservation hazardous forest fuel reduction treatments, primarily from the Deschutes and Ochoco National Forests. The increase in power that WSFPI produces will allow them to pay more for a bone dry ton of woody biomass. For example, WSFPI is currently paying only $10/bdt for woody biomass material delivered. When the current condensing turbine is replaced with the new extraction turbine, WSFPI will be able to pay about $25/bdt of woody biomass delivered.

WSFPI has undergone many changes since its birth in 1967. Larry remarked, "Their management is constantly monitoring our progress to be certain that we remain a benchmark for the timber products manufacturing industry and a valuable asset to the Tribes. Sustainable forestry, sustainable communities—that's what Warm Springs Forest Products Industries is all about."

White Mountain Stewardship Contract

In August 2004, the USDA Forest Service awarded Future Forest, LLC, the White Mountain Stewardship Contract on the Apache–Sitgreaves National Forest in Arizona.

The Apache–Sitgreaves National Forest, which comprises a significant portion of the largest contiguous ponderosa pine forest in North America, faces large-scale threats to communities from large wildland fires. The suppression of fire over the past hundred years contributed to the development of very dense forests. These forests that once were characterized by 20 to 60 trees per acre now average more than 400 trees per acre, which makes the forest vulnerable to intense wildfire and insect damage.

This project is the largest 10-year stewardship contract in the nation. The contract allows for the treatment of about 15,000 acres per year, up to 150,000 acres in 10 years. The stewardship contract also facilitates the development of a wood products industry better suited to market the excessive number of small-diameter trees on our national forests. Results include healthier forests, enhanced rural development, and utilization of previously unmarketable small-diameter trees and woody biomass.

Two individuals merit special recognition regarding the White Mountain Stewardship contract: Elaine Zieroth, USDA Forest Service Supervisor on the Apache–Sitgreaves National Forest, and Bill Greenwood, Eagar, Arizona, Town Manager.

Without Elaine's persistence, patience, and dedication to this process, the White Mountain Stewardship Contract would have never come to fruition. Bill Greenwood was born and raised in the White Mountain area and is very active in the community. He works closely with local agencies and businesses to improve forest health and create jobs, and he is dedicated to seeing the White Mountain Stewardship project succeed. Both Elaine and Bill continue to keep close tabs on the stewardship contract and are always there to offer their assistance.

The designated contractor, Future Forest, LLC, is providing services to perform woody biomass management, which may include tree removal, treatment of existing slash and dead trees, erosion control, resource protection, and haul-road maintenance. Future Forest, LLC, was formed by W.B. Contracting and Forest Energy Corporation to pursue this stewardship opportunity.

Because of the size, complexity, costs, and urgency of the task at hand, Future Forest, LLC, is engaging many other forestry and forest product entities in the White Mountains and elsewhere as they move forward to create healthy forests. The following wood products businesses in the community are currently receiving and successfully producing value-added products from material removed as a result of the White Mountain Stewardship Contract. Their stories are told in following pages of this document.

- W.B. Contracting
- Forest Energy Corporation
- Reidhead Brothers Lumber Mills Inc.
- Cheyenne Log Homes, Inc., doing business as Arizona Log & Timberworks
- American West Structures, LLC

What is Stewardship Contracting?
(Source: USDA Forest Service http://www.fs.fed.us/)

Over the past two decades, the Federal timber sale program has declined while the need for restorative work or maintenance in ecosystems remains. Some of the project work includes watershed restoration and maintenance, road obliteration for sediment control, wildlife habitat improvements, fuel load reductions, timber stand improvements, and insect and disease protection.

To accomplish the USDA Forest Service's stewardship responsibilities, creative approaches are needed to complete the necessary work and simultaneously contribute to the economic growth of local and rural communities. "Stewardship End Result Contracting" is one solution to this problem.

Stewardship contracting includes natural resource management practices seeking to promote a closer working relationship with local communities in a broad range of activities that improve land conditions. These projects shift the focus of Federal forest and rangeland management towards a desired future resource condition. They are also a means for Federal agencies to contribute to the development of sustainable rural communities, restore and maintain healthy forest ecosystems, and provide a continuing source of local income and employment.

In February 2003, the U.S. Congress authorized the USDA Forest Service and the Bureau of Land Management (BLM) to implement stewardship contracting for a period of 10 years. Some features of the authorizing legislation include allowing USDA Forest Service and BLM to apply the value of timber or other forest products removed as an offset against the cost of services received, apply excess receipts from a project to other authorized stewardship projects, select contracts and agreements on a "best value" basis, and award a contract or agreement up to 10 years, which may stimulate long-term investment in the local community. The authorizing legislation is found in the 2003 Appropriations Act (16 U.S.C. 2104 Note).

W.B. Contracting, Inc.

Implementing healthy forest restoration on Ted Turner's ranch in northern New Mexico is just one of the many jobs W.B. Contracting has on their reference list. Owned and operated by brothers Ricky, Dale, and Dwayne Walker, W.B. Contracting is a well-established wood contracting business that has been working in the Southwest for 18 years.

W. B. Contracting was formed in 1985 as a brush-thinning and slash-clearing operation, using small dozers and chainsaws to pile the brush. In the early 1990s, they realized that investing in mechanized small-diameter logging equipment was necessary to stay competitive and for their business to grow. So when they had an opportunity to buy some equipment (HydroAx cutter and clean wood chipper) from a local company that was going out of business, they did.

For the next several years, W.B. Contracting grew and prospered by moving their operation close to the market.

Dwayne said, "At first, this required us to move to New Mexico, but after 3-1/2 years we were able to come back to the White Mountains of Arizona, working exclusively on tribal lands, selling wood chips to the Stone Container paper mill and sawlogs to the Fort Apache Timber Company. However, in the spring of 1988 when the paper mill quit taking raw fiber, we purchased a feller–buncher and a stroke delimber in order to bid on a 3-year contract near Vermejo, New Mexico. In late 2001, that contract ended and we were able to move back one more time to the Arizona White Mountain area where work was again available."

All three brothers were born and raised in the White Mountain area. Ricky Walker is the President of W.B. Contracting, Dale is the Vice-President and Secretary, and Dwayne is Vice-President and Treasurer. Brothers Ricky and Dale are active full-time equipment operators or foremen on all forest restoration projects. The youngest of the brothers, Dwayne, participates in all decision making for W.B. Contracting but has also recently assumed a full-time position with Future Forest, LLC.

In 2004, W.B. Contracting partnered with Forest Energy Corporation, a local wood pellet fuel manufacturer, to form Future Forest, LLC, the prime contractor for the White Mountain Stewardship Contract (see p. 21).

"The right equipment is critical in our work," explains Dwayne. "We are continually looking to buy state-of-the-art equipment that operates on a variety of forest terrain." With the combined knowledge and experience of these three brothers, they are also quite capable of redesigning equipment if it is not commercially available.

W.B. Contracting, Inc.
P.O. Box 411
Eagar, AZ 85925

Dwayne Walker, one of the three brothers who own W.B. Contracting, Inc.

500-acre wildland–urban restoration project, Woodland Lake Park, near Pinetop, Arizona.

In 2005, W.B. Contracting received a grant from the USDA Forest Service National Woody Biomass Utilization Grant Program (see p. *v*) to purchase a versatile whole-tree log forwarder.

According to Dwayne, "A whole-tree log forwarder allows us to harvest acres that were previously inaccessible, thus reducing the number of new or reconstructed roads and landings. This piece of equipment has better weight distribution and less potential for ground disturbance and compaction than skidders. We hope to fit the forwarder with harvester heads that create a three-in-one felling, processing, and transport machine. This further reduces the number of passes that the equipment has to make over a site."

Dwayne's current job site is a 500-acre wildland–urban interface restoration project, Woodland Lake Park, near

Grapple skidder operating on restoration project.

Pinetop, Arizona. This forestland is on the Apache–Sitgraves National Forest and is part of the White Mountain Stewardship Contract. Wildland–urban interface areas comprise about 80% of this stewardship contract.

Several acres at this site have already been treated, and it was amazing to see the improvements they had made to this wildland-urban interface area. As I looked over the site and made favorable comments to the brothers, you could see in their faces the pride they have in their work and the gratification they get from doing it.

W.B. Contracting has a clear mission—to be the most successful, efficient biomass harvester in the Southwest. They are committed to making the White Mountain Stewardship contract a model for future stewardship projects in this country.

However, they also know that their company cannot do it alone, nor do they want to. W.B. Contracting is definitely a team player. They are active members of the Arizona Sustainable Partnership and Northern Arizona Wood Products Association that assist in marketing and small business development.

Dwayne spends a great deal of his time seeking out and helping to bring in new markets for the harvested forest restoration material. Since the White Mountain Stewardship Contract was awarded, new businesses in the area have emerged, such as a post and pole operation and a small-diameter sawmill. New companies that are on record as either in the process of beginning an operation or looking to locate in this area include a custom log home business, a power generation plant, and a chemical wood hardening company.

Among the three brothers, W.B. Contracting has 100+ years of experience in woodland operations and treatments, with a specialty in forest landscape restoration. The brothers have strong ties to the White Mountain community and have earned the respect of other local businesses in the wood industry. They have a reputation of delivering wood material for processing on time and within standard specifications. W.B. Contracting is a successful business not only because of its superior land stewardship ethics but because they know how to effectively collaborate on projects and build vital partnerships within the community. W. B. Contracting is well on its way to achieving its mission of being the most successful, efficient woody biomass harvester in the Southwest.

Forest Energy Corporation

The owner of Forest Energy Corporation looks forward to accumulating most of the wood residues in the area. When he buys it, he dries, grinds, and compresses it into small-sized pellets for fuel. Only a small component of this wood resource comes from sawdust, shavings, and fines left over after processing trees for lumber and other wood products. The majority is obtained directly from restoring forest ecosystems or reducing fire hazard in surrounding forests.

Rob Davis is the owner and President of Forest Energy Corporation, which manufactures wood pellets for fuel, in addition to animal bedding, absorbents, and a 5-lb compressed wood log for use in fireplaces and wood stoves.

In the 1970s, when many countries were experiencing an energy crisis, the first wood pellet manufacturing plant opened in North America. People soon learned that wood pellets provide a safe, reliable, and clean heat. In the 1980s, the wood pellet residential market grew tremendously.

Rob started his business in Show Low, Arizona, in 1991, primarily because "The Southwest is home to my children and several generations before them, although there certainly were other reasons why I built in this area, such as taking advantage of the large volume of wood waste from the local forest products industry, the potential market in this area, and the increasing cost of fossil fuel."

Because of Rob's well-known expertise in the wood pellet industry and his interest in forest health issues, he is frequently an invited speaker at conferences throughout the United States. He is a Past President and Director of the Pellet Fuels Institute and a member of the Arizona Governor's Forest Health Oversight Council and Southwest Sustainable Forest Partnership Steering Committee, a member of the WGA (Western Governor's Association) Biomass Task Force and the Review Team of the Restoration of Fire-Adapted Ecosystems component of the WGA 10-Year Strategy Implementation Plan, Goal III. He is President of Forest Energy Systems, a company developing sustainable heating and cooling systems using renewable biomass fuels for commercial and industrial applications. Rob is also one of two partners in Future Forest, LLC, the prime contractor for the White Mountain Stewardship Contract (see p. 21).

General Manager Curtis Rogers gave me a tour of the plant when I visited Forest Energy Corporation. The company employs 30 people in their processing plant and consumes about 150,000+ tons of green wood per year.

Forest Energy Corporation
1001 North 40th Street
Show Low, AZ 85901

The wood pellet manufacturing process starts when loads of raw material arrive at the plant.

Forest Energy Corporation, outside Show Low, Arizona.

Raw material (wood residue) just arriving at the plant.

The material is stored and eventually transferred into an in-feed system where it is metered into a screen, which separates the chips from the sawdust. The chips are passed through a pre-grinder and mixed with the sawdust. The material then goes into the dryer, where it is dried to the proper moisture content. The sawdust is conveyed onto a screen, which separates the fine sawdust from the coarse material. The coarse material goes through a hammer mill to be reduced in size and recycled back into the system. The refined material is then metered into the die where the pellets are formed. The pellets are cooled and then conveyed into a storage silo. The wood pellets can then be packaged into 20- or 40-lb bags, or bulk delivered for central heating customers.

"We promote sustainable, efficient, state-of-the-art production of clean heat and power from our valuable biomass resources, industrial wood residues, and forest restoration projects. We call it home-grown energy," Curtis noted.

Wood pellets packaged into bags.

Wood pellet plants voluntarily follow standards to create a product that is consistent in content, density, size, and quality. Forest Energy Corporation takes great pride that they are known for producing a high-quality product. There are currently two grades of pellet fuel: standard and premium. The main difference between the two is that the standard grade contains more ash than the premium grade. Pellet manufacturers are encouraged to label their fuel and have it tested regularly.

Pellet fuel can usually be purchased at stores that sell building supplies, pet and farm supplies, and hearth appliances. The cost of pellet fuel depends on the geographic region where it is sold, whether it is in bulk or bag, and the current season. Usually, wood pellets cost about the same as a cord of well-cured wood and less than all fossil fuels. Pellet fuel is estimated to be only about a third the cost of electricity. A residential pellet appliance is capable of generating 10,000 to 150,000 BTUs of heat per house. An entire house can be heated by pellet fuel when the proper appliance is installed. Projects using commercial boilers up to 40 million BTU per hour are currently in the planning stages in several Southwest locations. All are automatically fed and controlled requiring only normal periodic maintenance.

Curtis explained, "To become more cost efficient, we would like to get to the point of bulk delivery of wood pellets. The consumer would never touch the fuel. You could compare it to how homeowners currently have their propane or fuel oil bulk delivered. The owner could have an enclosed bin for pellet storage and an automatic feeder would transport the pellets to the stove or boiler. We could deliver the wood pellets as we make them, reducing our storage costs. Eagar, Arizona's Town Hall is one example of where we are doing this right now."

The cost of heating continues to increase, and people are demanding alternative fuels. Wood pellets are becoming an extremely economical alternative. Rob expects that "the pellet stove will soon be joined in large numbers by pellet furnaces, central heating systems, boilers, and commercial systems."

Wood pellet fuel is a growing industry that has the potential to boost the local economy and create jobs, especially in rural communities. Forest Energy Corporation is a result of Rob Davis' commitment and dedication to his belief that all biomass residues, and especially those from sound forest ecosystem management, are a valuable natural resource, not a waste product. Their prudent use is necessary for a sound energy future of our nation. And, if by increasing the health of our forests, he can also help the local community by providing jobs and economic stability with a low cost, reliable heat, so much the better.

Reidhead Brothers Lumber Mills Inc.

Reidhead Brothers Lumber Mills, Inc., in Nutrioso, Arizona, is a third-generation, family-owned operation with markets already established for various wood products.

Terry and his brother Darrel own Reidhead Brothers Lumber Mills, Inc., which includes a remanufacturing plant in Springerville, Arizona, and a large-diameter sawmill in Nutrioso. In addition, Terry owns a molding plant in Snowflake, Arizona. In April 2004, Terry purchased the former Precision Pine sawmill near Eagar, Arizona, and leased the land from the city of Eagar. This sawmill is becoming a major processor of small logs from the White Mountain Stewardship Contract (see p. 21).

Since purchasing the small-diameter mill, Terry has been busy retrofitting and installing new equipment. In October 2005, USDA Forest Service Sawmill Specialist Rusty Dramm was invited for a technical assistance visit to this small-diameter mill.

According to Dramm, "Terry Reidhead decided not to install a chipper canter in the existing mill in Eagar. This is because the logs are opened up with chipping heads and that reduces the ability to recover high-grade lumber from the quality zone of the log. The design of this mill is based on a 4-in.-wide bandsaw scragg mill, a modified bull edger, and a trim saw. The log factory has a bucking saw and debarker. When Terry purchased this mill, he left the old 7-foot bandmill in place because it is in good condition and could be used if larger grade logs become available."

This sawmill also has a planer mill with a breakdown hoist, planer matcher, and a certified truck scale. The planer mill has been running since August 2005, and the small-diameter mill is scheduled to be running some time in 2006.

Dramm said, "This mill design is suitable for processing the anticipated log mix of small-diameter material. The choice of a scragg primary breakdown and secondary cant breakdown are good choices for small logs. Terry has made good use of the existing mill equipment and materials-handling systems."

Terry's small-diameter sawmill presently receives all of its supply from the White Mountain Stewardship Contract. When in full operation, Terry expects to produce 12 million board feet of lumber per year and employ 15 people.

Terry recently installed a new wood chipper at his mill. Right now they chip wood slabs and sell these chips to Forest Energy Corporation in Show Low, a wood pellet manufacturing plant location about 60 miles from the mill. Terry proudly explains, "We make use of all the wood; we don't waste anything."

Reidhead Brothers
Lumber Mills Inc.
P.O. Box 84
Nutrioso, AZ 85932

Mixed log supply from White Mountain Stewardship Contract.

Debarker and bucking station.

American West Structures, a wood business located very close to Terry's small-diameter sawmill, could be Terry's largest customer of small-diameter lumber if they were able to kiln-dry their lumber to the required 8% moisture content.

This past year, Terry and American West Structures got together and figured out a way to help each other. In 2005, American West Structures received a National Woody Biomass Utilization Grant (see p. v) from the USDA Forest Service to secure increased capacity to dry lumber to 8% moisture content. Rather than build their own dry kiln, American West Structures is helping to fund a dry kiln at Reidhead Brothers small-diameter sawmill.

By helping to fund the dry kiln, American West Structures can increase their small-diameter lumber supply from 20% to 35% and increase their payment to Reidhead Brothers Sawmill by $20 per thousand board feet. In turn,

Terry is able to pay $3 more per ton for the raw material from Future Forests, LLC, the general contractor for the White Mountain Stewardship Contract. Terry hopes to have the dry kiln in full operation by spring 2006.

Terry wants to keep both the small log mill in Eagar and the large-diameter mill in Nutrioso running. However, he is not sure that the supply is there for the large-diameter mill. "It's the old family mill, ya know." Terry's grandfather bought the large log mill in1939.

Dramm believes that "Terry's approach to mill design is on track and should support efficient processing and handling of the log mix feeding the mill."

This area is a community with a rich forest heritage, and Terry's family has been part of that heritage since 1913. He is dedicated to the health of the forest and the prudent use of the wood materials being removed to promote that health. "It's my hope that it all keeps going until at least 2013; by then it will 100 years of forestry for my family." Terry would like his son, Charlie, to continue on with the family's forestry businesses. "I hope that this is his future."

American West Structures, LLC

Steve Nicoll and his wife, Colleen, own and operate American West Structures, LLC. The company is located just outside of Eagar, Arizona, and right next to his brother Randy's log cabin and post-and-pole operation. American West Structures is another small-diameter business in the chain of White Mountain Stewardship Contract (see p. 21) partners that work to increase the supply for local wood businesses and improve the health of the forest.

Established in 1998, American West Structures is a successful and growing small-diameter business. It specializes in manufacturing and pre-assembly of glued-laminated wood trusses, pedestrian and vehicular bridges, and laminated log home packages. The company also provides pre-packaged headers (for doors, windows, and garage doors) and custom beams.

Steve has been manufacturing log, timber, and laminated architectural trusses for 25 years. One of the company's main attractions is its ability to make a laminated beam that spans more than 24 feet without support. American West Structures uses small-diameter wood as their main source of raw material and a unique horizontal finger jointing system, which provides added strength for larger structures.

Steve adds, "We also do tongue and groove re-manufacturing of 1 by 6s, 1 by 8s, 2 by 6s, and 2 by 8s for local lumber yards. Right now we bring in raw material from local lumber mills and from the Northwest and Southeast sections of the United States. Our goal is to use more local material."

The company also has a waste collection system and sells their wood waste to Forest Energy Corporation in Show Low, Arizona, a wood-pellet manufacturing plant located about 60 miles from American West Structures.

Just like any successful business, American West Structures wants to change with the times and improve their products as new sources become available. To do that, however, the company has two major barriers to overcome.

Their first barrier is the volume of lumber they need to dry locally. There is no local supplier available to kiln dry lumber to their required 8% moisture content. The second barrier is lost sales because American West Structures cannot provide laminated wood decking, which is one of the most popular choices for large open spans.

Steve said, "Customers prefer to buy the trusses and laminated decking from the same supplier. Currently, the closest manufacturer of laminated decking is in Montana."

American West Structures, LLC
2000 West Central Avenue
P.O. Box 2008
Eagar, AZ 89525

Construction of small-diameter building to house deck laminating press equipment.

Vehicular bridge manufactured from pre-assembly glue-laminated wood trusses.

In 2005, American West Structures received a National Woody Biomass Utilization grant (see p. v) from the USDA Forest Service to purchase deck laminating press equipment and to secure increased capacity to dry lumber to 8% moisture content. Rather than build their own dry kiln, American West Structures is helping to fund a dry kiln at Reidhead Brothers sawmill, another White Mountain Stewardship contract partner, where the kiln will benefit both businesses.

By helping to fund the dry kiln, Steve said, "We are able to increase our small-diameter lumber supply from 20% to 35% from the White Mountain Stewardship Contract. American West Structures currently uses about 450,000 board feet each year of local, small-diameter lumber for various wood products. As a result of the laminated decking presses and the increased dry kiln capacity gained through the National Woody Biomass Utilization Grant Program, we can increase our usage to 2 million board feet each year and increase our payment to Reidhead Brothers Sawmill by $20 per thousand board feet."

As a result of the dry kiln and laminated decking equipment, Steve said that they expect to increase their sales by 20% each year for the next 4 years. They also predict that they will increase their employment from 13 employees in 2005 to 21 by December 2007.

American West Structures structural laminated decking will be available in lengths up to 24 feet. Steve explained, "We can produce random length and long-length laminated decking from local softwood species such as Douglas-Fir-South, ponderosa pine, and various face species. The face is a sound, tight-knotted grade that is machine sanded to accentuate the grain and the growth characteristics of the wood. It is required that the lumber be kiln dried to 8% moisture content rather than the standard 19% lumber. This lumber is then laminated with a fully waterproof exterior adhesive."

As of November 2005, American West Structures had a good start on construction of the 30- by 40-feet dry kiln to be located at the nearby small-diameter Reidhead Brothers sawmill. The building that houses the new laminating press equipment is being built entirely from small-diameter material. The building and installation of the press equipment are expected to be completed by early 2006. American West Structures plans to be ready to start receiving and shipping orders for laminated decking by July 2006.

Few companies manufacture laminating decking, and trends show that this market will continue to grow substantially. There is no doubt that American West Structures will continue to succeed. They are a dedicated partner of the White Mountain Stewardship Contract, and they will not let their partners or their community down.

Cheyenne Log Homes, Inc.
doing business as Arizona Log & Timberworks

Located just outside of Eagar, Arizona, Randy Nicoll and his brother Keith own and operate Arizona Log & Timberworks, a division of their Cheyenne Log Homes business. Although not the principal contractor for the White Mountain Stewardship Contract (see p. 21), 99% of their wood supply is a result of this contract.

Randy and his four brothers were born and have lived most of their lives in this area. For many years, the entire family owned and operated a glued-laminated (glu-lam) manufacturing business, Nicoll Laminates. In 1990 Randy and his brothers branched out to start Cheyenne Log Homes, Inc., which specializes in custom log home construction. At that time, most of their supply for the log homes was purchased from the Fort Apache Timber Company in Whiteriver, Arizona.

Cheyenne Log Homes had about $2 million in sales in 2004. "We have shipped log home kits all over the United States, and even to Japan and Taiwan," said Randy. After the family glu-lam business was sold in 1995, Randy and Keith became the sole owners of Cheyenne Log Homes.

In 2002, Cheyenne Log Homes purchased post and pole manufacturing equipment and formed Arizona Log & Timberworks as a division of their log construction entity. Their intention was to create a sustainable and highly effective business utilizing small-diameter trees and round-wood to produce a family of competitive wood products.

Since it began, Arizona Log & Timberworks sales have increased each year. "Our biggest problem has been getting the small-diameter material that we need to produce our products," commented Randy. "However, since signing the White Mountain Stewardship Contract, supply has not been a problem for us." In 2004, Arizona Log & Timberworks did about $400,000 in sales. In 2005, Randy says it was closer to $650,000.

Arizona Log & Timberworks has eight employees working in the yard for them. Current small-diameter products include vigas, posts, log railings, gazebos, utility poles, and log rail fencing. To increase their product line and remain competitive, Randy recently partnered with a successful wood pressure treatment company, Simmons Wood Products in Maricopa, Arizona, and made plans to install a pressure treatment plant at Arizona Log & Timberworks.

In 2005, Arizona Log & Timberworks received a National Woody Biomass Utilization grant (see p. v) from the USDA Forest Service for assistance with their treatment facility. Randy explained that this project is adding value to his small-diameter product material, which in turn means he can

Cheyenne Log Homes, Inc.,
   dba Arizona Log & Timberworks
1990 W. Central Ave.
Eagar, AZ 85925

Gazebo built by Arizona Log & Timberworks, Eagar, Arizona.

Log rail fencing.

pay more for the raw material, and that ultimately helps reduce the cost per acre of forest restoration.

Dwayne Walker, manager of Future Forests, LLC, and principal contractor for the White Mountain Stewardship contract, says, "Arizona Log & Timberworks is now able to accept mixed loads instead of sorted larger diameter material. By reducing the amount of time spent on sorting the product to be delivered, we are able to reduce our cost significantly in the removal of the biomass material from the forest and increase our profit by using more of the smaller diameter material that is currently being chipped. This in turn allows more woody biomass acres to be treated."

Arizona Log & Timberworks is in the midst of purchasing a few acres right next to their current yard for the treatment facility. They hope to have their treatment facility up and running by summer 2006. Randy said that the facility will be unique to the western United States in that it will

Hand-peeled vigas.

Small-diameter log supply.

treat wood products from small-diameter trees using a borate-based chemical called EnviroSafe Plus™.

"This treatment results in wood products that are insect-free; rot-, fungus-, mold-, and fire-resistant; and durable. The treatment works especially well on ponderosa pine, which is the dominant species coming from the White Mountain Stewardship Contract. It is a clear treatment that doesn't stain the wood. The wood looks natural but can easily be stained by the user." Randy is counting on this treatment facility to increase his current market for wood decking, replacing cedar, redwood, or synthetic materials. He says it also allows more uses for pine siding, log railing, log rail fencing, and even whole logs for cabins.

Randy explained that this treatment facility can be used to treat material produced by other local partners of the stewardship contract, such as the Reidhead Brothers small-diameter sawmill (3 miles away), which currently has to send many of its finished products 200 miles away to a treatment plant, and American West Structures, for their treated log siding and laminated decking. With this treating plant, Arizona Log & Timberworks increases their the capability of producing almost 39 million board feet of treated material a year, operating at a 75% capacity level.

To be moderately successful, Randy said, "We need to treat about a semi-load of material per week or about 25,000 board feet. We hope to be treating about 3 million board feet a year after the first year. There is a huge market potential for this, and we have a major marketing campaign planned." Their marketing area covers about a 300-mile radius around Eagar. "People still want real wood if they can get it," added Randy.

Randy wrapped up our interview by telling me something that I had already come to understand—the camaraderie and noncompetitiveness among all those involved in the White Mountain Stewardship Contract. He said, "People in this area all work together. By ourselves we can't make it work; it takes everybody. I think you will see that we work together here better than anyone else does across this country."

Arizona Log & Timberworks has indeed created a sustainable and highly effective business using small-diameter material from the forest to produce a family of wood products. They are proud to be part of the White Mountain Stewardship Contract, and they have made a pledge to be a business that cooperates, collaborates, and partners with others in order to contribute to forest health and the economic prosperity of their communities.